The Quest of George

The quest of George is a journey
to discover the fruit of love.

By Darrell Muth
and the Urban Bridge Church community

www.UrbanBridgeChurch.com

Imagine
Publishing
.com

Published through ImaginePublishing.com, 3428 – 99
Street Suite 444, Edmonton, Alberta, Canada, T6E 5X5
www.ImaginePublishing.com by Urban Bridge Church
www.UrbanBridgeChurch.com

ISBN 978-1-897409-09-1 (paperback)
ISBN 978-1-897409-10-7 (e-book)

Dedication

To the Design team: passionate, funny, risk-taking Christ followers, your creative and collaborative input crafts something much more than one person could ever do on his or her own.

To the Urban Bridge Church community: you willingly and regularly submit yourselves to the inventive machinations of passionate, funny, risk-taking Christ followers.

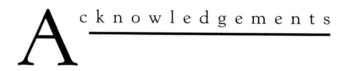

Acknowledgements

Thank you, Evelyn Giguere and Jalon Leendertse for creating the artwork for The Quest of George.

Thank you, Christian Schwarz for influencing our understanding of the fruit of the spirit of love.

Thank you, Tabea Gietz for both your concise and your compassionate editing.

Thank you, Dave Von Bieker for designing the cover.

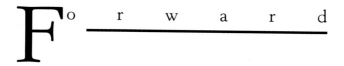

Forward

When Urban Bridge Church began in the spring of 2006 it quickly became very clear that creativity would be one of the central values of this community. Through music, in visual arts, during Sunday mornings and throughout the week we are very naturally a creative family.

One weekly exercise in creativity established early on in our existence was the Wednesday night meeting of our creative design team. From its inception it has been the role of the creative design team to shape the colour and content of Urban Bridge's Sunday morning worship gatherings. Over good food and great coffee about ten women and men discuss everything from how to decorate the stage area of our rented space, to what we should serve during the mid-service coffee break, and how we will convey the central teaching for the week. Traditionally teaching and preaching in most churches has been a solo project with the pastor or priest preparing their message alone, seeking God in solitude, and delivering the message from the pulpit on their own. Not that there is anything wrong with this solitary approach to preaching but over the last number of years we have been blessed and amazed to see God speak in the shared voice of the creative design team as we prepare each week's teaching together.

This is all shared with you the reader because the book you now hold in your hand is actually some of wonderful fruit from these creative design team meetings. Each chapter included here represents one Sunday's teaching for what became a summer's worth of story. Though some of the content and wording has been tweaked and modified for greater consistency and to better serve the printed medium the story is essentially unchanged from how it was originally presented to our church family. Of course, one may ask; "How does a Sunday morning sermon end up looking so much like a children's story book?" Well, perhaps we all read C.S. Lewis' "Chronicles of Narnia" one too many times. Or, perhaps we are just trying to follow in the footsteps of our saviour who "did not say anything to them without using a parable" (Mark 4:34).

Whatever the case may be, this story is part of our mythology, it is an allegory for and about our community. So as you read the pages ahead you are reading a story from Urban Bridge Church and you are stepping into the story of Urban Bridge Church. We recognize that just as our community is one small part of the greater story of the body of Christ so this short tale is one small part of the story of Urban Bridge Church. Our one prayer as we share the Quest of George with you is that in some small way that you will be inspired in your journey of faith in the same way that we were inspired to write it.

Happy Trails!
Tim Bratton, creative design team member

Introduction

About this book:

The Quest of George is the tale a farmer named George. Dissatisfied with the fruitfulness of his land and frustrated with life George believes that if he can farm land worthy of his efforts he will be satisfied. His quest for fruitful land propels him on a journey to petition the Great Land Owner. The journey exposes him to the qualities of love referred to in the Bible as the fruit of the spirit. These qualities are: joy, peace, patience, kindness, goodness, faithfulness, gentleness, and self-control.

About Urban Bridge Church:

Our faith community thrives in an atmosphere rich with artistic expression, rooted in the uniqueness of each member. We believe that our creativity originates in God, and from this origin we too create new things. It was in this setting that we came up with the idea of not just imbedding stories in our weekly Sunday communication but actually creating a narrative that would be the message. The result is an allegory that tells of the fruit of the spirit of love; The Quest of George

Darrell Muth
Pastor, Urban Bridge Church

The Quest of George— *Patience*

Ouch! Pulling the thorn from his hand, George slowly and deliberately squashed the offending weed under the thick padded sole of his boot. He enjoyed the act of defeating the prickly little enemy, knowing full

The Quest of George

well this quick growing weed would be back to torment
him all too soon. Thistles... why so many thistles? Why
didn't his vegetables and berries and bushes and fruit
trees have the same persistence? Instead, they reacted
resentfully to his efforts. Drooping sullenly, and offering
him thin, wooden fruit with scarce juice that arrived
late, if at all.

Sometimes George could swear that they were
conspiring against him. In the first moments of
wakening, while he still had one boot in his dreams, he
could hear their whispering in the early morning breeze,
challenging him to invest more of his money and time.
More... more... more. More of him; more time, more
money, more effort.

George was not one to wait. Had never been one to
wait. He wanted results now!

It was this insistence on having his needs met now,
that had splintered his bond with Emma. A delicate
flower of a woman, it was that lingering, subtle fragrance
of her life that had first drawn him to her. But now, she
was no better than the prickly little enemy in his field,
responding to his demands with a feeble, self-protective
bristly resistance—so unlike the person he once knew.

And he slowly squashed her long-suffering nature
under his edgy, thick soul.

Love. Yes, George remembered those early days
when the fruit of love sprouted from their life together.
Love had the potential to soften George's rough
qualities as Emma's fruitful, satisfying existence sought
fertile opportunity to root in him. George took pleasure
in this tender woman who exposed good qualities just
beneath the surface of his life. These qualities had been
pulled, like so many weeds, by a severe upbringing that
indiscriminately culled both the good and the bad from

Patience

his life. George began to believe that their children could be nurtured on love. That opportunity ended when the life beginning in Emma's womb died. Some of George had died too, and he reverted to a harshness that garrotted the love between them.

What truly bothered George was that his mediocre farm was surrounded by thick, gleeful land, land that seemed to bear fruit as if all by itself. Trees that stretched happily upward, offering their golden produce to the sky. Perky shrubs, pregnant with berries that grabbed playfully at his trousers, marking them with their copious juice. Streams that gushed unselfishly to feed the land, abandoning their banks in exuberance. Soggy ground, with its rich colour that mischievously gripped the thick souls of his boots, daring them to squash the spongy irresistible life beneath.

George's neighbours assured him that their land was no different than his.

When George asked them for their secrets, they proudly offered up their remedies for a fruitful return. He would stamp his great thick boot, "No, there must be more. I already know these things. They take too much time, too much effort. There must be more you are not telling me."

"George, George," they would assure him, "the land is like humanity; it needs nurture and love to grow." "George," they said, "take more time to invest in what you have been given. Sometimes it does take longer than planned."

George needed a return now, not later. George wanted the benefit of the fruit now, not later. This is what he would do. He would insist on his rights, better land—that's what he needed. He would appeal to the Great Land Owner.

15

The Quest of George

He paced and panicked and created excuses for why he had heard nothing. Then, word came back. The Great Land Owner's personal messenger brought the news. In a thorough explanation so as not to miss a thing, the messenger spoke for the Great Land Owner, explaining the journey and the conditions under which George could appeal. George's great padded boot tapped an irritated song in sync with his mumblings of, "Quickly man—finish your words."

The messenger finished, and George was given a map along with the appointed time he was to meet the Great Land Owner. George thought to himself, I'll make the journey in half the time, surprise the Great Land Owner with the importance of my need for new land, and be tilling new ground in time for the next harvest.

Before first light, before his land awoke to whisper its unhappiness, before his wife could be cowed and crushed, George was halfway through the township.

Emma slept in that day, and her bent spirit began to straighten, and a hint of her subtle graceful fragrance began to emerge. She had lain awake as George prepared to go. Without opening her eyes, she knew his abrupt movements were matched with the impatient markings of his familiar grimace and rutted forehead. That image was heavy, pushing her into her bed and encouraging her to discard the cautious goodbye to George.

Today? Today she would do little but linger over her flower garden, loving each extended moment.

Under the blue-grey canopy of daybreak George turned out onto the lane. Striding deliberately, purposefully he soon moved beyond the familiar. It was new, this land beyond his home. What surprised him most was the abundance of the land. Great thick trees supported by trunks wider than his hoe stood tall. Generous boughs bending over the path to offer him the best of their fruit. At first, George had little time for this nonsense; committed to keeping a brisk pace, he brashly swept the giving branches aside.

George exercised little, was soft in the belly, and just as soft in his feet. His great soled boots were out of place. Where they excelled in the soft soil, they suffered on a hardened path. Enough already! Fat, squishy blisters rebelling against the foreign activity screamed

The Quest of George

their disapproval and pressed against his heels. George was compelled to rest.

He picked a spot where his feet could reach the stream. The soft moss welcomed his bottom—gently. The aged apple tree received his rigid back—tenderly. The leaves of the forest whispered a gracious greeting to the hurried stranger.

A peculiar, pungent, earthy aroma was the first thing George was aware of as he opened his eyes. He cursed, as he angrily realized he'd been asleep. George was concerned; the sun had traveled a long way. He stood stiffly, dizzy with the quick movement.

The pungent earthy aroma moved!

Surprised and a little afraid, George realized an ancient man was resting against the backside of the same welcoming trunk.

The pungent earthy aroma spoke.

The ancient voice resonated with a deep unhurried cadence. This intrigued George, and for the first time in a long, long while, he chose to sit and talk. The ancient's narrative meandered, covering farming, politics, religion, and distant lands he had visited—even about a long-ago meeting with the Great Land Owner.

And for the first time in a long, long while, George subdued his habit of ending conversations in withering abruptness. He was content to let the old man ramble on. The ancient's presence was comforting.

The sun was being pushed down by the moon, and both men realized it was time to find shelter for the night.

"Here. Take my flask," the ancient offered. "It holds a very special wine from my own orchards—orchards the Great Land Owner himself has blessed. It is a wine that must be savoured and sipped slowly in good company, and not before its time. It will refresh you when you need it most."

Savouring and sipping in good company was not George's style. "How soon can I drink it?" was all he could think to ask.

"When it is time," was the ancient's reply, and with that, he offered his earthy, soiled hand in goodbye and slowly trundled away from George.

Needing to make up for lost time, George forced his body into a quick stride. Soon, too soon, he was tired. Refreshing—that's what he needed if he was to make the next village by dark. Dismissing the ancient's caution as foolishness, George removed the flask from its strap, quickly pulled out the stop, and jabbed the opening to his mouth, drinking deeply. He was overwhelmed by the harsh, cutting liquid!

A sharp thistle poked deep into the soft flesh between his thumb and finger as he swayed crazily on knees and palms and retched, and retched. Folding to the ground like a creased stem, George realized he could go no further.

George took pride in making the most of his time and opportunity, criticizing those who squandered extra moments in lingering and laughter. Unknown to him, his impatient lifestyle had given him a deserved reputation for poor-quality work and unfinished business. Now, for the first time in a long, long while, he asked himself, "Must I always be in hurry?" and he cursed his impatience.

Enduring Love—Patience
People of patience value perseverance, right timing, and controlled anger.
People of patience are people of justice and mercy.

19

The Quest of George—
Kindness and Faithfulness

The spongy moss that hemmed in the road stretched to the trees like a lumpy blanket and cushioned George, as his noisy stomach and aching sides recovered from the retching and heaving. He fell into an uneven sleep. It was rare for him to sleep away from home, and the breeze and the crickets upset the comforting whisper of his own country woods. Still, he was able to drop into scattered pockets of deep sleep. In the last, deepest pocket, he and Emma were kissing. It had been so long, and in his dream, she was the way he remembered her in the beginning: gentle, subtle, caring.

She began to kiss his chin, cheeks, and forehead—big, wet, sloppy kisses, murmuring her love for him. It was an affection long pushed to the back of their relationship. Emma's murmuring was morphing into soft growls which, quite frankly, startled George. Her breath... how best to describe it? It was like dog's breath.

The big yellow dog dropped back to its haunches, pleased to have roused the man on the ground. He watched as the man sprang to a sitting position, vigorously rubbing—more like scraping—his face, at the same time shouting sharp, strange words while offering his feet in a crazy cyclical motion. He wanted to play! The big yellow dog obliged by grabbing the boots, first one then the other, as they were offered.

George collected his senses enough to jump to his feet. Swinging the wine flask and frantically shooing the biting yellow monster, he grabbed a stick and pitched it at the crazed animal. It missed high and to the right, clattering far into branches, whooshing to the undergrowth.

The big yellow dog responded in a second, bounding gleefully to fetch the stick. George grabbed a rock, knowing the creature would return to attack. It did, but with the stick in its mouth, stepping proudly with a waggle in its tail.

George's shaking slowly subsided. His weak shooing noises at the dog were useless. The dog continually bounded off only to return with unfailing reliability. George gathered himself and continued on the path, periodically jabbing the walking stick toward

Kindness and Faithfulness

his overbearing, overly friendly new companion.

It was more than a village, more like a town, and bigger than what he was accustomed to. George cleaned up as best he could. Unshaven and smelling vaguely of vomit, he did his best to wipe the moss from his trousers. Finally, quite pleased with himself, he began his descent down the gentle rolling slope of the broad valley, unaware of the trapped piece of brown peat bouncing lightly where his coat collar met his matted curls.

Making his way to the edge of the town, he tried one more time, "Go! Go, you cur!" The big padded sole of George's boot aimed for the yellow dog's head but instead found its way into the beast's mouth, and the pooch gleefully wrenched George's leg like a turkey wishbone. Angrily, a bouncing George swapped a stick for his boot.

It really was a pretty town: everything in its place. An oversized sign welcomed George to "Benignus," and beneath the funny sounding name was a slogan that read, *"Welcome friend. Your home for a night or a lifetime."* A crisp banner strapped to a street lamp flapped in the breeze, quite unlike the frayed relics that clung to the lampposts of his own village. The town was larger than his, but not so big that a stranger would go unnoticed. George felt noticeable, but not in a comforting way, and he could tell by the townspeople's footwear that they did not farm. His big boots… common, tough, and useful in his region with their oversize great soles, drew attention to themselves. They looked menacing compared to the shiny tops and

The Quest of George

razor-like soles of the townspeople's shoes. George compared his rumpled, rougher appearance to the folk of Benignus. Like their shoes, they were finer, more sophisticated, more suited to life in Benignus than George could ever be. The cobbled stones continually grabbed at his toes, reminding him of the boots that were out of place.

At first everyone seemed friendly enough, nodding and smiling, just like home. But it wasn't like home. There was a difference. But what was it? George did not belong here. He knew it, and they knew it. Publicly, they welcomed all. Personally, they preferred those who were like them, or at least who tried to be like them. George was not. Ah, yes, they were smiling with their mouths, but their eyes, their eyes weren't smiling. Their eyes were evaluating him, measuring him. Back home, George treated strangers as he was being treated, but it was different now. Now he needed help. Perhaps if he initiated, it would be different. "And a happy day to you," he confidently offered the pretty young mother and bright, blond little girl. The woman reminded him of a younger Emma. The little blond girl giggled, and the mother smiled—but not with her eyes… just like Emma. The girl reached for the big yellow dog, and her mother jerked instinctively, pulling her back. "He's not my…" Oh what was the use? George had forgotten about the yellow creature padding reliably at his side. At least the dog's smile was genuine, trustworthy.

It was odd to be considered odd.

The Benignus town hall was new and placed prominently. North across the street was the court house, and to the northeast through the intersecting street was the post office. A large church had its home directly to the east. With its commanding presence, it

24

seemed oversized, even for this town, and George could tell that it was an important place.

The town hall was modern. Here and there were devices he had seen but could not name and machines he had never ever seen. A tall, wooden rack held rows of fancy folded paper. The sign said, "Take a brochure." George guessed that "brochure" must be a big word for fancy folded paper. He took one. The words on the brochure were written in his language, but they seemed to mean something different. It reminded him of the time he learned a new sport and the way he needed to understand the new jargon before the game made sense. It had been worth his while to learn the new sport. He was not sure if this was worth his while.

A big voice called from corner, "Hello friend." George turned. He had to be the friend, as he was the only one in the room. A thin, smallish man, with narrow shoulders and pants hitched uncomfortably high, owned the big voice. He wore the same shiny-topped shoes. Like the others, the man smiled, but not with his eyes. George returned the smile and wondered if his eyes also gave away the truth. The big voice continued, "Nice dog, but he really should be tied up outside."

"He's not..." Again what was the use?

"What was that?" asked the big voice.

"He's... he's not well trained," George replied. He impatiently swung the door open, and the dog obediently rambled out.

"You look like you could use some help, friend," the big voice offered. The man continued on before George had a chance to respond. "We'll get you some new clothes and a belly full of food in no time. Of course, we do expect a little consideration in return. What you need is to feel better about yourself, gain back some self-

The Quest of George

respect."

The big voice dashed to a closet in the corner and flung it open, revealing rows of brooms, shovels, and dustbins. Neatly stacked, worn gloves rested on a shelf above the brooms, and over that, another row displayed hats—each with a sign tucked in the headband that proclaimed, "By helping others, I help myself." The big voice smiled, stood on his tip toes, and reached for a hat.

George's eyes got big. He wasn't smiling. Now he understood. George was a threat. He might upset their orderly existence. George either needed to belong or to be useful. George, accustomed to measuring others, had himself been measured and found inadequate. The big voice spoke for the town. George did not belong. Therefore, he better be useful. George was angry. It was one of the few emotions he cultivated and, though not

mouth smiled, and her eyes smiled
and kindness and grace reached
deep into George's soul

Kindness and Faithfulness

productive, like a bristly weed, it bullied its victims into respecting him. George's big boot was readying itself for a stomp.

Landing butterfly-like, the touch was so light his impatience and anger brushed it away. But the touch persisted, not in a commanding way, but in a caring way. He shifted to see an elderly woman. Her subtle fragrance reminded him of the best of his wife, and the large sole eased up. She smiled, and her eyes were listening eyes, caring eyes. They were kind.

"Karl," she directed her herself to the big voice, "how about I take over from here?"

Karl replied, "Friend, you go with Charis. She'll take good care of you."

"My, what a friendly dog you have!" Charis was taken with the big yellow dog as it marched beside George. "What is his name?"

"His name," George said with resigned acceptance, "is Ubaid."

"And does he live up to his name?" Charis asked.

"Yes, if nothing else, he is faithful." George smiled.

Charis, George learned, was from somewhere else but had lived most of her life here. She once was married to a man from Benignus who met her on his travels. But the love of her life had died many years ago. Upon his death, she learned an unkind truth. In the absence of her husband, she no longer belonged. Charis was devastated by the loss and loneliness. She began to shrivel in her spirit, and her capacity to love slowly yielded to a ravenous bitterness. Her loneliness and heartache demanded an outlet, so Charis had become a town hall helper to break the monotony, to dull the hurt. Charis told George of another stranger passing through Benignus long ago whom she had also taken in. He

27

The Quest of George

showed her a deep kindness and planted the same in her, reviving the fertile blossom of her life. He was, she later learned, the Great Land Owner, who often travelled in disguise to better know the land and people. She told George that something remarkable happened after her encounter with the Great Land Owner. Even after he left, his spirit remained in and around her.

Charis offered her full attention to this new stranger with the out-of-place footwear, and the brown peat dangling at the nape of his neck. She fed him; she cleaned and pressed his clothes, and even wiped his boots. All the while she listened, and her eyes gently drew out memories, the good ones sliding easily off his tongue, and the hard ones, once drawn out like a stubborn sliver, lost their power to inflict pain. And when he spoke of his quest, she nodded.

He knew she knew how he felt.

He felt safe with her and asked her opinion of his need for new land. She replied that, not being a farmer, she couldn't really know. But she encouraged him and said that the Great Land Owner surely would do what was best for George.

Refreshed and encouraged, George was up early enough that a lamp was necessary. Charis had wrapped and packed him enough food for a number of hearty meals, placing his flask on his carefully folded coat to ensure George would not forget it. He told her its story, and she encouraged him to keep the flask, remarking that right timing often had to do with a right heart. George was less sure.

The one thing he was not sure of was the offer of

Kindness and Faithfulness

her dead husband's boots. They were finely made solid boots with high lace tops to protect his ankles and firm-gripped soles; they were ideal for his journey. Though they were more suited to the farm than the road, George liked his own boots. Although he would not admit it, he needed them. Thick and padded, with the ability to stomp out threats, they represented his life in so many ways. Take the boots, she offered, "You don't have to wear them just yet, but take them."

George agreed. He opened the closet to gather them up and noticed three sets of boots: his great-soled, thick boots on the left, the high-topped, firm-gripped boots in the centre, and on the right, ancient and dusty from their long rest in the closet, another pair of boots—just like his. "Are these...?" Charis simply smiled, and her eyes smiled, and kindness and grace reached deep into George's soul. George and the big yellow dog made their way down the dew-saturated path leading out of town.

Amiable love—Kindness
Reliable love—Faithfulness
Kindness expresses itself through the simple details
of life and relationships: being interested in others,
showing attention, listening, remembering the little
things, being tender-hearted, and forgiving.
In a word, kindness is grace lived out.
Have you been one to show kindness?
Faithfulness speaks of reliability and
trustworthiness—consistency that can be counted on.

The Quest of George—
Peace

George had taken his time crossing the valley towards the rounded green and grey peaks. They fenced the valley with its town and grassy range. His hard-pressing pace flagged, as he took in the strange smells and sounds of a landscape unlike his own. A bold river divided the valley, and tributaries spread from it like the

The Quest of George

fingers of a great blue hand, each finger sparkling with diamond-like brilliance. Some of these were shallow enough for him to ford by strapping his boots to his pack and hiking up his pants. Others teased him to try, but George quickly discovered they were too deep and too swift. Fortunately, sturdy bridges carved out of grand planks painted in brilliant hues of blue offered him a safer, drier passage.

The big yellow dog made no distinction between shallow and deep, catapulting into the wet with rambunctious yapping. The first time caught George by surprise. Soaked by the splash, he cursed—a sound so incongruent it tainted the air, displacing the peace. And in response, a perfectly timed gust of pristine air filled in the space.

He remembered the first time he had cursed at Emma and how her head had snapped as though struck by the cruel comment... how her eyes had expanded in hurtful surprise. Later, he had mumbled an apology of sorts, being careful to balance it with his commitment to make sure Emma knew where he stood. George, with fresh understanding, now knew that those harsh words were the chisel that helped crumble the peace they had enjoyed.

The quest was giving George time to think about his character, and what he saw was not always pleasant. Intuitively, he knew there was a better way to live. He had seen it in the lives of those touched by the Great Land Owner, and now it seemed that the land itself was speaking on His behalf, calming George's spirit, replacing anger with peace.

George had misgauged the distance across the valley to the range, and now, late in the day, George struggled with the steep grade. The great, leafy trees that had shaded him protectively, were handing him off to unfamiliar pines. The higher he climbed, the more obvious the hand-off, and George became more unsettled. The familiar continued to give way to the unfamiliar. Even the smooth, earthen black path lost ground to a new trail with varicose veins of roots that hurt George's feet and shale that tested him as it shifted under foot. The dead man's boots slapped loudly but uselessly on George's pack.

The higher he climbed, the cooler it became. With each rest stop, his sweat immediately chilled him. George had never been this high up; he was concerned. The next town remained at least two hard days walk away. George thought he had prepared for sleeping outside; he was less sure now. He was surprised at how quickly the sun was running to hide behind the mountain. The sense of well-being and calm that had carried him from the town across the valley was lifting. In its place, he felt agitated and uneasy, with a sense of unnamed foreboding.

And now this. The path was breaking into three— the left path headed partially west and north, the middle almost due north, and the right more east then north. It was hard to see in the low light. Had he missed a sign?

Unable to go forward and knowing it was too late to turn back, he felt despair. Despair's dark hand bullied him to the ground. At least the big yellow dog had remained true, and for the first time, George stroked its broad head, scratching firmly on the fur covering the hard bone behind the dog's ear. The big beast leaned in grinning, forcing George to brace with his free hand. The dog groaned and yawned, and George offered a cautious smile. This untamed terrain had its own sounds. Imagined or not, the sounds made the near

The Quest of George

darkness even less appealing.

He readied an undersized fire and pulled out a sandwich prepared by Charis of Benignus so many hours earlier. Reaching for the flask, George hesitated. Was this the right time to drink from it? George certainly needed refreshing, and it seemed like a good time to enjoy it… Yet, he couldn't afford to become sick again. The ancient had also told him it was to be savoured in the company of others, and George didn't think the big yellow dog qualified as "others." George let the flask rest.

The dog noticed first. Its furry neck changed texture, and a growl thundered out of its belly. The dog gathered itself and pointed down the path. George gathered himself, crouching behind the dog, and grabbed his walking stick.

They were foot steps—heavy, deliberate—and a clink-like scraping sound accompanied the steps like a metronome: a walking stick, then a long pause. The fire's glare obscured George's sight, but he knew with helpless knowing that he was being observed.

Illuminated by the small fire, the man's size was exaggerated by his shadow silhouetted against the brush. The figure seemed monstrous as he made his way to George. "May I?" the figure asked, motioning near the flame to a spot across from George. George hesitated and nodded his uncertain reply.

A broad, soft-brimmed tweed hat and grey jacket, the kind George wore for his chores, covered the large-boned man. These were worn and soiled, creating a gloomy match with the patched, dark twill trousers and old brown shoes. The man stretched a leg to the fire, exposing a hole in the sole and leaving a grey-socked foot unprotected. His big, crevassed hands with their

protruding veins were stamped with dirt. He looked like
a drifter to George.

"You don't belong here do you?" the man stated as
much as asked.

"No," George said, with finality, not wanting to give
anything away to the drifter.

"I have a place one day's walk north of here. If you
don't mind, I'll stay the night." George did mind. But
what could he say? The man looked suspicious. Not the
kind of person George normally associated with.

The man made several attempts at conversation but
George wasn't interested in small talk. Drifters begged
instead of worked and stole from honest, hard-working
people. His father had taught him this, as he had taught
him how to deal with drifters. For now, he only wanted
to get through the night. Soon, both lay down to sleep.

George awoke several times, but the darkness was
complete. He could only hope he would be safe until
morning. He felt for his pack, the flask from the ancient,
and the extra boots from Charis. The big yellow dog
pushed against him, offering some reassurance. George
regretted ever leaving his farm.

The switch from sleep to waking was swift, and the
peace he felt in his dream drained away immediately,
leaving the dull residue of dread and anxiety in his gut.
The dog was gone! He grabbed to his right. His extra
boots were gone! George cursed as he had not cursed
in a long time—a long sentence of disconnected vulgar
words, all directed to the dark man in the soft-brimmed
tweed hat, the drifter.

George was on his feet, his walking stick in his grip.

The Quest of George

When he found that drifter, he would teach him a lesson never to be forgotten.

But which path? It didn't matter.

The dog pushed through the bush like a plough horse and playfully glanced off George's knee, almost knocking him to the ground. From the same direction followed the dark man in the tweed hat. The man's whistling reached George first, and then he spotted the hat. "Why, you!" George shouted, "Where are my..." George stopped. The man had a heavy string of fish in one hand and a pair of highly polished boots—George's boots—in the other.

The man's whistling stopped. "I caught some fish for us for breakfast, and your boots... they are fine boots. I appreciated your hospitality last night and polished them using a black root, the way my father taught me."

Shame was an uninvited and unfamiliar feeling. George was ashamed. He was ashamed that he had mistrusted this man. Ashamed that he had intended to hurt him. Ashamed of his past and of a father who taught him to take, not give—who taught his son that wise men were former foolish men who had once trusted and then learned a bitter lesson.

The fish were fine. And the man... He was not nearly as large as he had appeared the night before; he was no bigger than George. In the absence of shadows, the man's features were softer, even gentle. And when he smiled, his eyes smiled.

George learned things about the man, and he learned things about himself. He learned that the man, his name was Lewis, had not been as frightened as George. He had been taken back by George's apparent lack of welcome, but trusted that a man with a friendly dog must have more good qualities than bad.

They continued their journey together. Lewis was a woodsman, a logger who earned enough to care for his family. What surprised George was that he did not have his own land, nor did he feel the need to. Instead, he lived by a great river. What caused George to ponder more than anything else was the contentment he sensed in Lewis. His clothing was poor, he earned barely enough to survive, and he did not have his own land to work. Yet, he was at peace with himself. That calm affected George... so much so, that he did something foreign. He apologized without excuse for how he had treated Lewis the night before. Lewis smiled, and his eyes smiled. Even George smiled.

According to Lewis, his inner calm had not come naturally. He had lived a rough life, a life learned from his clan. He had robbed and beaten a man and driven him off his land, then moving onto it himself. One day, a traveller arrived with a small party and asked for lodging for the night. Lewis planned to rob them too, and drive them away.

He didn't—he couldn't—and instead, Lewis came face to face with the traveller who seemed to know all about Lewis's past and how he had come by the land. Lewis thought of running away, and he could have, but he was touched by this person who treated him with dignity and respect, though he didn't deserve it. He told George that something remarkable happened, that even after the stranger left, the man's spirit remained in and around Lewis.

Lewis returned the land and made restitution. He was forgiven. And in being forgiven, he accepted what he was and made a promise to treat others as he had been treated. Since then, he had. Later, Lewis heard

The Quest of George

rumours that the Great Land Owner himself had passed through his county, and he wondered…

They came upon the place almost by accident. The excited, delighted call of Lewis's wife and squeals of his brood pulled George into the moment, and he laughed as he had not laughed in a long time.

The place itself was where he could picture the Great Land Owner living. It was perfect. The immense

river idled along with its magnificent emerald caste. The
edge was gentle and shallow. Huge oak trees lined its
banks, and in the boughs of the grandest tree, Lewis had
built a simple home.

And here George was at peace.

Later that day, George placed the solid, firm-
gripped boots at the feet of Lewis—who rejected them,
insisting that George would need them for the journey
ahead. He looked at George's great thick-soled boots
and smiled, and George smiled. The boots, of course, fit
Lewis's feet perfectly.

George could see his reflection in a clear, still pool
isolated from the river. Bending, he peered closely at his
reflection. "Who are you George?" he whispered.

He could see his reflection in the scuffed mirror of
his home… impatient, demanding.

He could see his reflection, surprised by kindness,
in the basin provided by Charis. Now he saw a different
George and thought to himself, what will the Great
Land Owner think of me?

The Quest of George

Reconciling love—Peace
Peace is a reconciling quality of love.
Peace is found in actions and attitudes of
reconciliation.
We need to reconcile with ourselves, accepting who
we are—both the good and the bad.
We need to reconcile with others.
We need to reconcile with God.
In these reconciliatory acts, we discover
contentment and peace.
Peace isn't dependent on the actions of others; it is
dependent on us.
Peace is what we give to others, and it returns as a
gift to us.

The Quest of George—
Self-Control

"Who are you George?"

"George!" Lewis called. Captivated by the image in the pool and the calmness of the river, George, embarrassed, clambered the bank to Lewis who was holding a book. Dark brown and bound in a simple but sturdy manner, Lewis placed the book in George's

The Quest of George

hand. "It will help you remember your journey and organize your thoughts."

It was a journal. George's thanks were sincere. He understood the sacrifice it was for Lewis and his family to gift him. George's emotions were conflicted. He considered writing and reading for leisure to be wasteful. He placed the book alongside the flask, adding another weighty item to carry. Still, he respected Lewis and would attempt to honour him by using it. After all, Lewis trusted him and was providing for him.

Lewis and Bess, his wife, welcomed George to stay with them till the end of the season, which was now coming to completion. Besides, they wanted him to meet their eldest daughter, Mary, who was returning home from a journey. George, who had generally shunned close relationships, was humbled to be considered a valued friend. But he had another motivation for lingering. He had planted a garden—yes to help with food and to keep active, but also to see if he could farm well under different conditions. After all, he was a farmer, though not a very good one—until now.

The garden grew! It grew vigorously! Vegetables in a rich patina of greens, oranges, reds, yellows, and browns poked their leafy tops through the soil, as if all by themselves. Vines heavy with fruit begged for the sun. Cabbages, lettuces, and corn conspired with their leafy colleagues to make George a success.

The dark earth by the river taught George something that had escaped both him and his father before him.

He could not demand or force the land to grow.

He could not discipline the land with his punishing hoe.

He could not motivate the land to produce more

simply by adding more.

George learned a simple truth that season. The garden responded best to love: straightforward, disciplined actions of consistent and careful tending of its needs.

Mary surprised George. He expected her to look like Bess, who, though lovely in character, was homely. Mary, unlike her mother, was not. Mary also surprised George by paying attention to him. She admired his garden and loved his stories. She listened.

George felt complete, and in this completeness questioned the need to continue his quest. To be a successful farmer, he need not leave the river. He was with people who respected and liked him. He also considered his life with Emma. Weighing the dissatisfaction he felt on the farm and balancing it with Emma's disappointment in life, he considered that it might be best if he remained here.

George also thought about Mary and how a life with her might look. He understood that these might not be reasonable dreams. Would Lewis and Bess want their daughter to be with a man who had abandoned his wife and past, who lacked the discipline to complete what he had begun? Regardless, for now he would be unreasonable and dream of what could be, not what should be.

Ubaid, who one would think should be content, was becoming dissatisfied with this peaceful life by the river. Anxiously barking and continuously pacing, George would trek the surrounding valleys in hopes of calming him, but no sooner would George turn back than the big yellow dog would again become agitated, criss-crossing George's path, attempting to herd him away, not back.

With the garden complete and Lewis about to

leave on an extended journey, it was decided that they would have a celebration. The night before the party, George had a dream. He was hoeing the garden which had grown so thick that when he traveled down a row, the tangle of green blocked the sky. In his dream, he paused, proudly reflecting on his success. Behind him, footsteps padding in the moist soil stopped. Though he could not see her, he sensed that Mary was right behind him. He allowed the moment to wrap itself around him, waiting for her to tell him how proud she was of him. Mary placed her hand on his shoulder. Unexpected but welcomed, George was tense with anticipation of the forbidden. Turning to embrace her… he faced Emma. He awoke. George pushed hard against the memory and dream of Emma. He had found land that produced and a woman who admired him. Why couldn't he remain here?

The meal, complemented by George's vegetables, was wonderful. Mary, in a beautiful dress made for her in a distant place, was lovely. George was convincing himself that remaining was the right thing to do. There was one more thing that George could do to complete the evening. George decided that now was the time to share his wine. He repeated to himself the conditions the ancient had given him. It must be drunk at the right time and in the company of friends. These were more than friends by now, and as far as he knew at that moment, he would never leave that house. He recalled Charis's wisdom of right timing being of a right heart. Who was to judge another's heart? He dismissed the advice.

Self-Control

George surprised the family with an unexpected shout, "A toast!" Cups were raised, salutations given, and wine taken. The joyful moment deteriorated into disgust. The wine was sour. Vile, red liquid spewed from mouths, and George vomited on Mary, ruining her dress.

Mary left the room, stained. Bess, her hospitality strained, began to clean quietly. Lewis sat in silence while George, embarrassed, offered rambling apologies while he packed. In all of this, only Ubaid seemed pleased, his haunches shivering and tail wildly waving at the mouth of the path.

They moved determinedly through the night. As quickly as he moved forward, his mind raced back and remembered Emma. He remembered the parts in her he thought were Mary. A fire shed enough light for him to journal his sorrow and his love—for Emma.

With the clarity that often follows crisis, he knew for certain that he must honour the commitment the Great Land Owner had made to him and complete this quest.

Disciplined love—Self-Control
To have self-control is to have power over oneself.
But self-control is not an end; rather, its goal is to serve others better.

The Quest of George— *Gentleness*

Chilled air splashed against George's face as he pushed on. The dark made things worse than they really were. It was good to walk. Walking helped straighten the worrisome kinks that tangled his mind. It was true that he didn't leave Lewis and Bess under the best circumstances. Until he allowed undisciplined thoughts to overtake him, he had never experienced such peace as

The Quest of George

he had at their home.

George's memory of his last moments with Lewis and Beth was too fresh, still raw. He had begun to clamber down from their soaring tree house when that familiar thick boot planted itself a heel's width from his nose. George had winced involuntarily, almost expecting the menacing toe to boot him the rest of the way down. It is that kind of justice that the boot had applied in the past to those who had crossed George. But the boot was on a different foot, Lewis's foot. The boot had remained rooted in its place, obedient to its new master. Instead of lashing out, Lewis had folded his sturdy frame over George, grabbed George's shoulder and squeezed. George looked up to face the man, and Lewis smiled, and his eyes smiled.

He was making good time in his new footwear. The inscrutable flask from the ancient bounced a rhythmic tattoo against his pack, and his big yellow companion, Ubaid, was content to amble. The path led him alongside the immense emerald river. Its unchanging presence slowly seeped into his spirit and helped muffle the anxious voices within.

The moon's light had hinted at changes in the setting, and the new morning revealed the full picture. The valley was slowly opening into an immense expanse of ground. George was startled, even a little afraid. He had listened to travellers describe a territory called prairie, but until now, he had spent his life cocooned in the brown and green of woods and valleys, in turn held in place by sloping hills and framed by distant greyish peaks. In George's infrequent reflective moments, he pictured a cosmic gardener tending the countryside which was his home. He saw no evidence of the same in this unruly mass.

Gentleness

Like a vast dry lake, the colour of his favourite string bean, bluish-green knee-deep grass swelled and rippled in the dry wind. It reached as far as he could see. The sky covered the expanse, a great blue bowl fastening itself to the prairie somewhere beyond. The flat land was empty of trees except for occasional canopied clusters, and George felt exposed, vulnerable, and insignificant. Tiny. The path thinned to a dry trickle as George pushed the walking stick ahead of him, uncertain and lonely.

The wind found a new voice in the grass, like a reedy whistle, reminding him of his neighbour Happy who could whistle through his teeth and smile at the same time. George chuckled. What he would give to hear Happy whistle.

Ubaid heard it first, a sharp sound that jabbed through the air. "What is it boy?" George called, hooding his eyes as he scanned the ground. The big yellow dog answered by bounding to his left and stopping like a sentry about a hundred paces away. This time George heard it, the whistle of a human, and he followed the sound to two distant figures moving towards him. They were closing in rapidly.

They loped towards him, and at a distance, it seemed as if they were skimming on top of the grass. Tall, trim, and warrior-like, their hair was the colour of corn. With eyes blue like the sky, they slowed to a walk as they closed in. They were a woman and a man. He had never seen people like this. George squeezed his staff, and Ubaid, parked by his side, was neither friendly nor disinterested.

The woman spoke. Her voice was calm and sounded like music. George didn't understand a word. She spoke again, noises that were more guttural, like she was

The Quest of George

trying to clear her throat. And again, George did not understand. A third time she spoke, "Hello."

"Hello" George replied.

The woman continued; "I have not spoken this language in a very long time. Do you come from the south, where men fence their land and farm the rich dark soil?"

"Yes, I do," George responded.

The woman said, "I admire those who can grow life from dirt." My name is Metea, and this is my brother, Cathmore.

Cathmore cut in, "Sister let me speak for myself. What is your name, where are you from, and where are you going?" challenged Cathmore.

"I am George—and where are you from, and where are you going?"

Metea laughed, "Perhaps we have found someone who likes to argue as much as you, Cathmore."

George learned that they had come from a land far to the west and had been exploring for a long time. They too were heading north to the country of the Great Land Owner. When George explained his quest, they offered to travel with him. George, after a moment of hesitation, agreed. Trust was still new to him.

Though they were brother and sister, they differed in temperament. Metea was mild-mannered, calm, and seemed genuinely interested in what George had to say. Cathmore's belligerence emboldened George. He asked Metea how she came to be so different from her brother. Metea told the story of meeting with someone whom she would later learn was the Great Land Owner. Travelling alone, she had been stalked and attacked by two men wanting her money and more. Cornered and injured, she was still prepared and capable of defending herself.

Gentleness

She spotted a third figure walking deliberately towards them. Metea, knowing she could not fight off three, was in despair. The stranger was not their companion. He saved her life, but with calm and gentleness rather than force. Afterward, he salved and bandaged her wounds and helped her to the next village. His presence was profound, unforgettable. She told George that something remarkable happened after her encounter with the Great Land Owner. Even after he left, his spirit remained, in and around her.

Cathmore argued with his sister on almost every point, and it wasn't long before George and Cathmore argued. It was Metea who ended one particularly long debate. "Enough already. I have never met two more self-righteous, intolerant people in all my life."

The movement on the horizon was a welcome change to the endless grass. At first, it was just brown shapes moving. The shapes gained form as the trio closed in, and the welcome became alarm. Back home, George had his own cow and was familiar with the deer that raided his garden, but these creatures were neither. Black-brown in colour, with broad faces and deep chests, the creatures blocked their path. Their piled, heavy muscles twitched and stretched their almost hairless skin. Dropping their massive heads to chew, jets of dust sprang off the ground from the force of their breath. They were again as large as the largest cow, and their curled horns made them seem even bigger. One beast with a broken horn looked in their direction, raised its head, and snorted.

Cathmore hardly slowed his pace. "If we have to go

The Quest of George

around this herd, it will add at least a day to our journey. George, lend me your dog, and we'll see what these beasts are made of."

George opened his mouth, but it was Metea who responded, "Cathmore, we need to slow down and think this through. Your bull-headed fighting ways have gotten us into enough trouble in the past."

"Metea, you may be beautiful and courageous, but you have the nature of a lamb," was Cathmore's quick response. "If I can't take the dog, then a brush fire will clear a path for us. The wind is in our favour.

Metea caught her brother. "No, there must be another way..."

It would be risky, but in the end, George and Metea agreed on a plan, and Cathmore had no choice. George held the three straws. Cathmore drew first; it was uncut. He was safe. Next, Metea drew, and the straw slid out of George's loose fist. George saw that it was he who was holding the short straw. His task required courage, gentleness, and calm—qualities George had tried to remove from his life. Metea paused, smiled, and her eyes smiled. Shifting her fingers she took the short straw.

She walked slowly and steadily into the herd. Moving closer and closer, she moved until she could touch, even smell them—the odour of sweat, dung, and wet grass rising in a steam from one of the creature's backs. It raised its head, snorted, and pawed. She stepped forward again, and the massive head with its small black eyes returned to grazing. Metea caught the eye of her companions, offering a sure nod.

George walked ahead very slowly. Ubaid, sensing George's nervousness, remained close to his thigh. George's legs went heavy; he fought his panic. He could see Emma and their home and orchard, and he regretted many things. He wondered why he had felt so strongly to press for more.

George wasn't sure how long they spent quietly passing through the herd, but after a while, his heart gave up its fight with his ribs. They continued among the massive creatures.

George felt good about himself that night as the three settled by the fire. For the briefest moment, George considered pulling out the flask with its remaining wine—after all, it was a time to celebrate, and he was in the company of new friends. "No, George," he counselled himself. "I don't think so. I'd sooner take another chance with that herd."

In his new journal, George wrote that he had, for most of his life, despised gentle, humble characteristics as feeble and things to be pruned. Yet today, he had been saved by them.

Serene Love—Gentleness
Gentleness is a humble love.
It is the opposite of argumentativeness, self-righteousness, stubbornness, and the need to win.
It is calm, tranquil, and serene.
Yes, there is a time for the tough love needed to fight for what you believe… But more often than not, there is a time for gentle love. Gentle love is the rule, not the exception.
Its qualities are mildness, tolerance, and humility.
Gentleness can be risky.
Gentle people risk being misunderstood, overrun by aggressive actions, and hurt by intolerance.

The Quest of George— *Goodness*

The three trekked hard. Metea and Cathmore with their long-reaching legs, hardened and practiced, moved in fluid tempo. George discovered that the rhythm of life extended beyond planting seasons, coaxing his arms and legs into a coordinated motion to keep alongside. Once again, he whispered a prayer of gratitude for

The Quest of George

Charis's gift of boots. He placed his hand gently on the broad yellow head that nodded at his side. He was less grateful for the silver-capped flask clicking a repetitive reminder on the brass ring of his pack.

The plain seemed to extend beyond the horizon and, though none of them complained, they were tired of the monotony of featureless, swishing grass. Cathmore's sporadic shouts of, "I see something!" each ended with a curse at the trickery of cruel mirages.

It ended so quickly, they nearly tumbled, and even gentle Metea shouted in surprise. The plain was, in fact, a plateau. Its end was marked by a definite drop-off. The land before and below them was spread with farms, like rectangular earthen throw rugs in earthen shades of yellow, brown, green, and black—each fringed with a fieldstone fence. A thread of thick, blue water was woven through the centre.

The rugs of earth matted the entrance to an enormous city. "City" was Metea's word for it, for George had no word to describe what he saw. He saw masses of ornate structures, like a rich man's garden, complete with row upon row of varied, colourful buildings. The thick, blue thread of water flowed down its middle, and bridges clasped the two sides together. George studied the silver and copper roofs intently. Each roof grabbed a fistful of sun to throw his way.

"It is so bright!" was all he could say. The city was fashioned like rings of circles flowing out from the middle, each ring had a road that connected and defined that circle. In the middle was a large square, and in the large square was a building that drew all attention to it. It pulled at George's eyes. The entire city seemed to bow to the centre.

"This must be it; this must be where the Great Land

Goodness

Owner lives," declared George. "What do you think Metea, Cathmore?"

"No," they responded together, in rare agreement. Cathmore continued, "Metea and I have heard rumours of a city which is before the place of the Great Land Owner. This must be it. If we are correct, it is named Briet, because it shines so brightly." He continued, "We have also heard stories that it is not all it appears to be."

"What do you mean?" George responded.

"Only that, for all its beauty, all may not be as it seems," Metea offered. Cathmore followed up quickly, "Metea, we will not pass through this place," and again, Metea agreed.

"You are right Cathmore. We will continue on."

George was just as sure. "I am going to the city of Briet. Perhaps I'll meet another like Charis. Metea, Cathmore, I have come to appreciate you as more than travelling companions; you are my friends. Cathmore, you remind me of myself, and there is good in that."

Metea pulled George to her and whispered, "Be careful friend. Hopefully, we will meet again."

Metea and Cathmore smiled in goodbye, and their eyes smiled. Then, with an abrupt start, their tall strides separated them from George.

George chuckled to himself, thinking of his plain farm and earthen village. The only evidence of dirt in Briet was in clusters of hanging plants. He wished Emma was with him to enjoy this. George had once witnessed the birth of a two-headed calf, but even that was topped by the wonders of the city of Briet.

Opulent was one word that kept coming to George's

The Quest of George

mind. Everything was opulent in Briet. No trim was
without paint, leather shone with fresh oil, and the
cobbled streets were ornately patterned. Carriages
rushed by; their inlaid precious metal trim shouted,
"look at me," and paired horses in expensive harnesses
stepped with fine breeding. George didn't have to
worry about standing out. The wealthy citizens of Briet
were much too focused to notice George, except once,
when Ubaid used a newly painted lamppost to do his
business.

"New" also described Briet. Fresh concrete sent
its wet odour past the large screened fences that
camouflaged construction. George recognised the
muffled working sound of hammers and saws. Even the
people looked new in their shiny shoes with razor–like
soles—as in the town of Benignus—but finer, much
finer. And when the people smiled, which seemed to
be a regrettable exception, their eyes didn't smile at all.
Still, George's first impression was that life was very
good in Briet. But was it?

George looked up, way up. A giant face, taller
than his largest orchard apple tree was painted across
the brick and was staring right at him. It was a very
handsome grinning face that said, "Mayor Arman
invites you to dinner." The backdrop for the giant face
was the centre building of Briet. Dinner was for that
very evening, and there was an open invitation for all
new-comers.

His best shirt was far from the best shirts worn by
the others, yet he wasn't out of place. The square in
the centre of Briet, which could have swallowed up his
home village, had drawn all manner of men and women,
both elegant couples and plain folk. There were many
races. George thought he knew why he was here and

wondered about the others.

The voice came from his left. Loud and clear, but not offensive, it was rich and cultured, and it compelled him to listen—stopping just short of commanding him to do so. George could make out the form of Mayor Arman, high above the crowd, speaking from a platform, which itself was in the shadow of the most beautiful building he could imagine.

"Welcome to my home, and welcome to Briet—the best place on earth."

George found himself cheering along with the rest, every eye attentive and chins slightly raised and forward. Arman continued, "Like so many before you, you are on your way to the home of the Great Land Owner. It is a worthy goal, and the Great Land Owner has much to offer. But perhaps what you want is not to be found there. And perhaps, just perhaps… you will find your desires, all the good you can hope to gain and achieve, here. Let me explain." Arman did explain, and by the time he finished, it was dark. But no one seemed to complain or notice. The crowd cheered wildly, and the people made their way to the tables of food and drink.

It sounded so good and so right. If not for his journey's experiences and the caution of Metea, George might have been tempted to stop short of his quest for the Great Land Owner and instead invest his life in Briet, which according to Arman, would give him 100 times the yield of the best land available. It was tempting. There was one other thing; his faithful companion the big yellow dog was agitated, and George had learned to heed Ubaid.

George ate quickly and formed a plan for the evening. He must tour the magnificent house of Arman.

The Quest of George

It was beyond his experiences and beyond his imagination—beyond anything he could dream of. The house of Arman was overwhelming. George considered how his life could be different if he followed Arman. He moved from the entranceway. Noticing a large frowning man posted further in the antechamber, George slipped to the right and followed the corridor. Ubaid's clicking nails surprised George and he realized he would need to find a less open space, but there were no doors, only alcoves.

The movement startled him; it was a flash of cloth and a door clicking to close. George reached, but the

Goodness

door disappeared into the bare wall. He leaned against the wall and kicked it in frustration. It gave way, and he landed hard. The corridor was dark, small, and it smelled not of opulence, but evil. A slight, skinny woman recoiled, pressing into a corner. She was about Emma's age, George thought, but she seemed older, weathered and grey like a fence post.

"You cannot be here. You cannot be here!" She was nearly incoherent, bunching her sack-like dress in a knobby fist. "Leave this house. Leave this city while you can!" She continued, "I was once like you but look at me now. He asks for you to invest your money, then your time, and then he takes your soul. There are many like me. He owns me; he owns my soul. How can I return home? I am in debt, and I am disgraced. I serve in this house, but most work the mine behind the hill half a day to the south." She paused, then said, "There is more. Leave this evil place." As she pivoted to scurry down the gloomy corridor, something dropped. At first, it appeared to be a bark chip, but looking closer, George could see it was a scale.

The Great Land Owner had been specific about when George was to meet him. If he left Briet now, he should have no trouble making the date. But he was troubled. Were the rumours true? George had almost been convinced to remain in Briet. Once again, he had contemplated dropping his quest and giving up on Emma. George had to see for himself if it was possible to appear to be good, yet to be so evil. He had been befriended by so many on his quest whose good actions had helped him. Yet, he still seemed to have the capacity to be selfish, himself evil. How evil could a man become?

It stung him hard, piercing his heart until it ached

The Quest of George

and bled with the admission that his quest had really
had one purpose—to have more. He had abandoned his
wife and left his farm, sad as it was, in a quest for more.
Was he any different than Arman? George needed to
know.

Grey clay neutered the landscape of all potential
for life. The farmer in George was appalled. But that
observation was minor. In the bluish-black sky of early
dawn, he could see heads emerging from the ground.
It was a deep pit large enough to swallow a good-sized
lake, and it was infested with moving bodies. Humans
with picks, shovels, and sacks strapped to backs; there
were too many to count. They too were grey and devoid
of hope.

"You what!" The voice from beyond the weathered
shed startled him. It was the voice of Arman—a very
angry, very evil Arman. Ubain growled. It came from
deep within and both startled and assured George.
They ran to the shed and slowly made their way to
the voice of Arman. George poked his head around to
follow the voice. What he saw caused his leg to shake,
and he sank to the ground. The voice came from an
evil that momentarily froze him, pushing him to run
away. Arman had taken the form of the evil that he was.
George looked again. A dragon-like beast had forced
two women against the shear edge of the pit. George
could make out parts of terrified words, "My child…
sick… need time." The women gripped one another,
swayed, and then fell as Arman slashed at them with the
serrated edge of his clawed wing.

George was running, "No, no, leave them alone!"

Goodness

Arman turned. The yellow eyes and foul odour terrified George. Still, he ran toward the beast. Arman pounced, pinning George to the earth. The wing with its edge was sweeping downward just as Ubain, in frightening yellow fury, leapt and clamped onto the beast, missing its throat but catching the joint where the shoulder intersected the wing. Arman screamed and pitched, the dog flaying like a rag. George rolled away from the fighting forms, scrambling to his knees just as the beast planted its good wing for stability. It pinched George's fingers to the ground. He cried out, pulling away. His baby and ring fingers were missing. His wedding ring gleamed in the clay. The beast attempted to rise into the air but the dog's grip had made its wing powerless.

The beast clawed and ripped at Ubaid. Still, the big dog hung on in unwavering persistence. George had to do something, had to help. A discarded shovel with its broken handle lay against the shed. George sprinted to it. Turning, he saw that the beast and the dog were balancing on the edge of the pit. With his good hand, George hurled the spade. End over end, it arced and then planted, the spade imbedding itself in the beast's neck. Yellow puss-like blood exploded outwards and the combatants toppled, disappearing into the gloom.

On his belly, George inched to the edge. Peering into the gloom for his companion, George could only see that it was deep, still, and dark. Angry voices were coming closer. He picked up his ring and stumbled into the gloom, running until he felt safe.

Then, he wept.

The Quest of George

Correcting Love—Goodness

Goodness is in opposition to all forms of evil—in
others and in ourselves.

It is a measure of God's correcting love.

Sometimes we do need to be harder on ourselves.

Goodness begins with correcting things in our own
life.

Have you ever had to take a stand?

Have you ever met evil and known it?

The Quest of George— *Joy*

He knew he should be feeling sadder about things, maybe even feeling sorry for himself. His hand was heavily bandaged, wrapped in clean strips of cloth to protect the stubs where his two fingers were missing. George deeply missed Ubaid. George would respond, by instinct, to yellow dog rustlings. But he was disappointed by counterfeit noise of the wind and rodents, mimicking his faithful companion.

The Quest of George

Still, even the jarring ox cart he was on, multiplying the pulsing pain in his injured hand, couldn't bury the seed of joy finding life in his spirit. This was a strange feeling for George—to be happy, content in difficult circumstances. If only Emma could…. oh, Emma would. She would listen to how he had overcome so many difficulties and had learned things about himself. She would hear him say how sorry he was and how much he loved her. This was George's promise to himself and to Emma. His journal had become a truthful testament to this change. He prayed it wasn't too late.

The happy reasons for his present state sat on the raised box at the head of the cart. Two sets of broad shoulders wrapped in simple cloth blocked his view of the team of oxen drawing him nearer the Great Land Owner. Mr. and Mrs. Elder, or, as they insisted, Sardis and Beatrix, had come upon George in the forest as he lay recovering from his escape. Half carrying him, the husband and wife moved him deeper into the woods, away from the awfulness of the mine with its pit, away from Arman, and away from the big yellow dog.

Their story burrowed deep into George. A long time ago, they too had been on their own quest to meet the Great Land Owner. But the city of Briet, with its energetic broad streets and wealth, had diverted them. Finally, Arman's promises had deceived them.

Once their money was gone and their usefulness worn flat, the Elders found themselves slaving in the mine pit. They had each other and lasted longer than most, but their end was inevitable. But one day, they were distracted by cursing and barking. The guards were trying to drive away a dog, and they had succeeded. But the large dog was persistent and

66

returned to the pit repeatedly. Placing its paws near the
edge, its bottomless rich bark would echo over the yawn
of the abyss, and again the guards would drive it away.
If Arman was present, his abuse would overlay the
landscape like a cursed blanket. That persistent barking
presence pushed back the desolation in the Elder's lives
enough to give the couple an idea. They would find a
way to share their food with the dog.

They found a moment and sneaked to the spot
where the dog always came. Bending to place the food,
they were confronted by the big yellow animal. With
hands of mouldy bread extended, they pursued him.
Finally, when the dog paused, they were far from the
pit. They simply continued on. The big yellow dog
disappeared, and they became part of a loose network of
rescuers.

"A big yellow dog? Tell me more about this dog!"
The abrupt intensity in George's voice startled the
couple. Passionately, chaotically George squeezed and
pulled at his rescuers' memories. Pairing their encounter
with his, George believed they were describing Ubain
and from this belief grew hope and more joy

Best of all, they told George of the Great Land
Owner. When they did, they smiled, and their eyes
smiled.

Beatrix would end each story with the inevitable,
"and George, he is so handsome," to which Sardis
would respond, "Aw, woman, I wouldn't know about
that, but he is a man's man." Then they would laugh
loudly, gleefully, and Sardis would run that large paw of
a hand over his face, rubbing the tears into submission.
George absorbed the laughter, occasionally releasing it
with a giggling snort, and the hilarity would continue.
Yes, he should feel sadder about things, maybe even

The Quest of George

sorry for himself, but he didn't.

"There it is!" Beatrix's unlady-like voice bellowed George awake. "Can you see the tower?"

He could. The tower was the first sign of the Great Land Owner's home, and it drew the ponderous oxen towards it a half-step more quickly. A lake pushed against the city from the west side and wiggled its way to the city core in a network of canals. George, the farmer, had trouble comprehending the way the land surrendered such a variety of life: fruit, vegetables, shrubs, grass, and trees impregnated every inch. An array of carelessly spread pools and small lakes contrasted the green. George was so captivated by the scene that he almost missed the colossal vine-covered arch marking the city's entrance. Passing beneath it, he exclaimed, "Who built this arch?"

"It is not an arch," was Beatrix matter of fact reply. "It is a bridge." Indeed it was.

George could not let go, "Why build a bridge where there is no need?"

"There once was," she responded, as though he should know this, and then she shared the story.

"There once lived, in another time, an ageless man. He was not a young man, for his face bore the wrinkles of a wisdom gained over time. But he was not an old man either, for his body was still full of vigour, and his mind was rich in imagination.

"The man lived in a land inhabited by many other ageless ones. It was a good land, full of life. No one owned anything, because everything was the property of the Great Land Owner—and no one was in need of anything, because the Great Land Owner freely shared everything. The ageless man had lived in this good land for so long and enjoyed the refreshing water and great food of his land for so long, that he often forgot any other lands existed.

"There were other lands, many of them not so good. In fact, in some of the other lands, there was great drought. There, with every passing year, wrinkles ran much deeper, bodies grew much weaker, and the hearts of the people sought childlike joy much more often than they found it.

"The ageless man's land was actually an island. It was separated by a great expanse of water from all the other lands. And so, it was quite easy to forget the other lands existed—quite easy, until one day when the ageless man was down at the water fishing. He had come down many times before and would return many times after, but this day was different. After a couple of hours, the man saw something coming on the horizon, foreign and at the same time familiar. He saw that the thing was really a person, a man much like himself, on a raft. Soon the raft was so close that the ageless man standing on the shore could see the deep lines in the stranger's face. The wizened man finally reached the shore and stepped off the raft and onto the beach where the ageless man had been fishing.

"The ageless man soon discovered that the land from which the old man had come was in a great drought. Immediately, he gave the old man all the fish he had, brought fruit and vegetables from his garden, and drew fresh water from his well. He sent as much as the old man could take back with him on the raft. The ageless man knew that what he had provided could only help a few people. The situation seemed so hopeless,

The Quest of George

but what could he do? The raft was so small. The ageless man promised that he would come to that dry land across the water.

"Not on a raft, but on a bridge.

"But who could build such a massive bridge?

"The ageless man began to plan. He spoke with engineers, carpenters, and builders of all kinds. They all told him that to build a bridge of that size was too difficult. It had never been done. The ageless man was discouraged and disheartened. He had only just begun, and already he had to abandon his dream, his promise.

"He tried to return to his normal routine and to forget about the bridge and the old man. But when he ate the fruit from his garden, his sweet strawberries seemed sour, and his apples were bland and boring. He no longer felt refreshed in his pool, and as he drank from his well, it would never quite quench his thirst. He was feeling the thirst of those from the dry land, and he needed to do something about it.

"Desperate, the ageless man decided that he must speak with the Great Land Owner and petition him to build a bridge across the waters; surely *he* could do this. Welcomed into the house of the Great Land Owner, the ageless man made his plea, asking the Great Land Owner if he would build a bridge across the waters to the land in drought.

"The Land Owner told the ageless man that he had wanted to build such a bridge but that no one had been willing to build it. 'Are you willing to build this bridge?' the Great Land Owner asked, pointedly. Unsure of his abilities but unable to shake his memory of the old man he had met on the shore, the ageless man agreed that he would build the bridge.

"'But how?' he asked.

"'I will supply all you need to build the bridge,' answered the Great Land Owner, 'all you must do is work.'

"So the ageless man began to build the bridge, uncertain of himself, but sure of the Great Land Owner's promise and the old man's need. Night and day, he worked on the bridge—alone. It took years. Eventually, he saw what the old man must have seen so long ago—the shoreline of another land. The ageless man cried out with excitement and called for others to come and see. When the others came to the bridge and saw the far-off land, they joined the ageless man in building the bridge. Soon the bridge was complete.

"The promise was finally fulfilled. With great joy, the ageless man ran across the bridge in search of the old man he had met so many years earlier. There was now food and water—and joy—enough for everyone.

"The landmass magically expanded with the population. As the land grew and flourished, the water separating the lands shrank, until people didn't even need to cross over on the bridge anymore."

George caressed the wedding band tucked deep in his pocket. He mused; *Things would be different if I had known of these beginnings: My farm, my life with Emma. Yes, things would be different—fruitful.* How would he ever describe this place to Emma?

The city was beautiful, though not more beautiful than Briet. It was large, though not larger than Briet. Yet, it was everything Briet was not. "Permanent" was one way to describe it. The city had been there for a very long time and provided a sense of stability, hope, and

The Quest of George

assurance—peace. There was something else... What was it?

George was experiencing a joyful, loving feeling. People were talking to one another in vigorous discussions, consoling intimacy, laughter, and direction-giving. Peering down the side streets, George could see a mix of intimate streets and courtyards, and with rare exception, doors were open, creating an inviting movement of bodies in transparent relationship. It was as though he was peering into their lives. And even in the haphazard intensity, there was a pervasive feeling of well-being. George himself was taken up in this same sense of security. He realized that, although he had perhaps missed his one opportunity to meet the Great Land Owner, he still needed to try.

Sardis pulled the cart into a stable. "This is as far as the cart can take us. Grab your things, George. We need to find the Great Land Owner. George grabbed the pack with his good hand and hoisted it over his back; the remains of wine in the flask swished a reminder of other, less joyful times.

"Where can we find the Great Land Owner?" George asked a shopkeeper.

"Hard to know. He is always about, but if you take this lane, you are sure to find him sooner or later."

Off they went, and at each turn, they would ask the same question. Each question resulted in the same answer. Through side streets, courtyards—even kitchens and gardens—they passed. In each case, their strange appearance and eager question was not an interruption. Poor Sardis and Beatrix soon realized their need to spend more time off the ox cart, so George slowed his anxious pace.

The lane opened into a very large courtyard. Its

size surprised George. Benches, gardens, random
groupings of chairs, and fish ponds filled the space. A
hum of animated conversation pulled George to the
large group in the middle. A young man and woman on
the perimeter were listening intently. George asked yet
again, "Can you tell me where I can find the Great Land
Owner?"

The young man seemed surprised by the question.
"Where? Here, and if you listen closely, you can hear
him."

George mimicked the response, "Here?"

"Yes, here," the young woman laughed.

George was suddenly very nervous, his ears felt
warm, and his fingerless stumps throbbed. "I am
on a quest, and I was to meet him but missed my
appointment. I… I need to speak to him. Who can make
an appointment for me?"

The young man shifted from George. Focusing on
the centre of the activity, he shouted, "Sir, a traveller
says he must speak to you!"

The hum subsided immediately, and in the
momentary silence, George felt equal parts elation and
dread.

"Does the traveller have a name?!" a clear voice in
the middle asked.

"What is your name?" asked the young woman.

"George," George whispered.

"George!" shouted the young woman. "His name is
George!"

"George," said the clear voice from the centre,
"come here!"

The mass of men and women parted as George,
Sardis, and Beatrix shuffled their way in. And each one
smiled, and their eyes smiled.

The Quest of George

The Great Land Owner was seated at a small round table. He stood. Yes, he was handsome, and he certainly was a man's man. But he was so much more. He hugged Sardis and Beatrix, which resulted in Sardis pawing away more tears. Then, he took George by the hand, pulling him close. He peered intently into the farmer's eyes and whispered, "George the farmer. You are late." He paused. "But not too late." And he smiled, and when his eyes smiled, George saw the virgin soil of joy.

The great hall was prepared for a banquet. Occupying the centre was an extended table. To George, just a simple farmer, it seemed set for a king. The Great Land Owner placed himself not at the end, but in the middle.

George was stunned by those he saw at the table. He scanned the room slowly, fastening a surprised gaze on each guest, who smiled in turn. And their eyes smiled. Each chair was occupied by someone who had helped him in his quest. To the Great Land Owner's right, the space was vacant except for a cushion on the floor. Next in line sat the ancient George had met on the first leg of his journey. Even here, the man's pungent earthy aroma was present. On the Great Land Owner's left, sat Charis from Benignus. Directly across, Metea and Cathmore waved and nodded. Sardis and Beatrix were to the left of the brother and sister, grinning broadly. Then, an enormous door swung open and in strode Lewis, with his great thick-soled boots, accompanied by Bess and Mary. George ran to meet them. Slowing as he neared, George gathered a hand from each and genuinely asked for forgiveness. After much weeping and hugging,

Joy

George was placed at the head of the table.

The sound of clicking on hardwood echoed against the stone walls. The sound drew near him, becoming familiar. Curious, George rose and half turned, only to be knocked down by a slightly limping, large yellow dog, his companion, Ubaid.

After the shouting, barking, and yet more weeping subsided, the dog took his place on the cushion by his master, the Great Land Owner.

"George," called the Great Land Owner, "let's deal with your most urgent business first." He continued, "You have come to petition me. Remind me, what is it you demand?" George had done it; he could not believe that he had completed his quest and that he was in a position to argue for his right to better land.

"My petition sir," he paused, "my need for more…" he stopped again, "… has been fulfilled."

"How is that?" was the Great Land Owner's intense reply.

"My quest, aided by the men and women seated here, is complete in meeting you. My land is fine; you have shown me that I am the one lacking. If I may, please allow me to return to my farm and to Emma, and I will make you proud."

"So it shall be. George will return to his land!" shouted the Great Land Owner. "George," he continued, "there is one thing I cannot give and that is Emma. If she will have you back, then she is yours."

"I understand," George replied. The ancient stood, "I propose a toast to George in honour of the completion of his quest—but we seem to have forgotten the wine." He smirked, "George will you provide the wine?"

If ever there was a perfect time to savour the wine in the flask, this was it. He was with the Great Land

75

The Quest of George

Owner and in the company of friends. It was a fitting time to refresh those who had helped him succeed in his quest and, yes, his heart was right.

He had wasted so much of the wine prematurely that there would never be enough to go around. "My ancient friend, the flask is all but empty."

The ancient was insistent, "Well let's pour what you have." And everyone at the table nodded. So George poured and he poured, and the perfectly aged wine, with its magical bouquet, refreshed and renewed his friends. As he drank, he was filled with love.

The Great Land Owner smiled.

As the Great Land Owner's guest, George spent much of his remaining time at the small round table in the large courtyard listening in silence as he observed the inspiring dance of life orchestrated by the Great Land Owner. George realized that he could be this example of the Great Land Owner to his people. He realized what he must do, and he knew where he belonged.

The journey home was completed with a sense of purpose. One unknown remained: Would Emma have him back? His friends, who accompanied him as far as their various departing points, advised him, coached him, and teased him. Finally, on the last leg, he was alone. George's resolve clashed hard against his insecurities.

Arriving at the border of his farm, the silhouette of the cottage against the darkened sky scared him. Inside, the light of the table lamp revealed an occasional shadow which he guessed must be Emma. Another slighter shadow confused him. He wrote in his journal, "This is so very hard. What now... what if she says no?"

Well, it was certainly too late to go on tonight, he reasoned. After all, there was no sense in frightening Emma. He would wait until morning.

George had become accustomed to sleeping in various places, but this night, he fell into an uneven sleep. He dreamt he and Emma were kissing. It had been so long, and in his dream, Emma was the way he remembered her in the beginning—gentle, subtle, caring.

She began to kiss his chin, cheeks, and forehead, murmuring her love for him. It was an affection long-ago pushed to the back of their relationship. Emma's murmuring was morphing into soft growls which, quite frankly, startled George—but her breath was sweet, just as he had remembered. He jolted to a sitting position! Emma clung to him sobbing and laughing, and a puppy with big paws and a yellow coat dropped back to its haunches, pleased to have roused the man on the ground.

It was a beginning. Things would be different now. George knew his life would now be fruitful—not because he had different land, but because he was different.

The end.

The Quest of George

Rejoicing love—Joy
The fruit of joy is a paradox. It most often finds it
expression in difficult times.
Joy results from two different actions:
One, joy is an expression of love that results from
living a life of peace, patience, kindness, goodness,
faithfulness, gentleness, and self-control. If you want
joy, then be and do these things.
Second, living fruitful lives does not guarantee a
happy outcome, but God tells us joy is not influenced by
the outcome, but by living fruitful lives regardless of the
outcome.
The quest of George is a journey to discover the
fruit of love.